For Laurene

Boating Cartoons by sacha warunkiw

UnderWay

. . . it all began
when CO2 met Oogak,
washing him out to sea
in the late Pleistocene epoch
of the Neogene period.

1

Published in Canada 2007
LONGDOG PUBLISHING
P.O. Box 170,
Milford, Ontario K0K 2P0
www.longdog.com

Library and Archives Canada Cataloguing in Publication
UnderWay Volume 1
ISBN 978-0-9782535-0-9

1. North American Boating - -1996-2007- - Cartoons.
2. North American wit and humor, Pictorial.

Cover Illustration by Sacha Warunkiw
Layout, Design and electronic Imaging by Printcraft
Printed and Bound in Canada by Shield Printing

The majority of the cartoons in UnderWay Volume 1 were first published in PassageMaker Magazine
from 1996 to 2007. The balance were published in DIY Boat Magazine or have not been published before.

We first met Sacha and his humor when we launched PassageMaker Magazine in 1995, when few in the industry recognized the growing interest in cruising under power. In the years since, however, Sacha has helped us explore, develop, and enjoy this lifestyle with humor, wit, and an incredible knack of seeing the fun in all aspects of the niche.

His own cruising experience gives him an in-depth understanding of the trials of boating, and the many ways we find to torment ourselves and our spouses when near the water. Sacha's comedy in cartoons reaches into our hearts, bringing smiles of "I've done that!" and "That's me!" to those who take it too seriously. Life is truly better than fiction, and his comedy showcases the non stop ways to poke fun at ourselves and the hilarious journey we call life.

— Bill Parlatore, Editor in Chief, PassageMaker Magazine.

WHILE WAITING FOR THE DELIVERY OF THEIR NEW TRAWLER MARC AND BETTY DREAM ON.

IT'S TOO BAD WE DIDN'T KEEP THE HEDGE CUTTERS WHEN WE SOLD THE HOUSE.

WHICH OF YOU IS THE CATCH OF THE DAY?

DIESEL REPAIRS: IF AT FIRST YOU DON'T SUCCEED...
BEAT IT INTO SUBMISSION!

11

I GUESS HE FORGOT HIS WHEELBARROW ABOARD!

"NICE.....NICE PAINT JOB PETE...BUT THAT'S NOT OUR BOAT!"

IN THE INTEREST OF PEACE AND TRANQUILITY ABOARD, THE CAPTAIN OF THIS SINGLE SCREW OFFSHORE PASSAGEMAKER PRESENTS THE FIRST MATE WITH A BACKUP "GET HOME SYSTEM".

DURING THE NIGHT FRED LET OUT A LITTLE MORE RODE.

GARGANTUA, GARGANTUA, THIS IS TINY TUNA. I UNDERSTAND YOU'RE HEADED FOR NEW ZEALAND ONCE OUT OF THE CANAL. HOW'S ABOUT BUDDY BOATING?

21

POSTCARDS HOME

23

AFTER 40 YEARS IN THE CORPORATE WORLD, HOWARD SETTLED INTO THE CRUISING LIFE ABOARD HIS TRAWLER.

"AFTER SELLING THE SAILBOAT AND BUYING THE TRAWLER WE DISCOVERED...WE NO LONGER NEEDED FOUL WEATHER GEAR!"

SATELLITE DISHES, INMARSAT, DIGITAL COMPUTER TELECOMMUNICATION, INTERNET, E-MAIL, SSB, HAM, VHF, CELLPHONE... NOW WHAT THE HECK WAS GOING ON BACK AT THE OFFICE?... IT WAS TOO QUIET!

UNKNOWINGLY THE DELIVERY CAPTAIN LEAVES NOVA SCOTIA
BOUND FOR BOSTON WITH THE CANADIAN STOWAWAYS.

34

OUR FIRST CROSSING AND YOU RUN AGROUND ON THE ONLY ICEBERG IN SIGHT?

"DON'T SHOOT TILL YOU SEE THE WHITES OF THEIR EYES!"

39

"DID WE EXPLAIN TO HIM THAT YOU'RE SUPPOSED TO LET GO OF THE ANCHOR WHEN DROPPING IT?"

EVER SINCE WE REPLACED THE SAMSON POST WITH A FIRE HYDRANT AND PLANTED GRASS, BOOM BOOM HAS BEEN A HAPPY PUPPY!

THE UNRULY GRANDCHILDREN STABILIZED, THE CREW GOT BACK TO ENJOYING THE CRUISE.

IT ALL BEGAN WHEN SHE COULDN'T FIND FRESH VEGGIES ON OUR TRIP TO BAJA.

FRANKLY, WE DON'T MIND BUYING YOU A BEER BUT PERHAPS YOU COULD SPARE US THE DETAILS OF YOUR ENCOUNTER WITH THE BIG WHITE WHALE.

IT'S A SALES GIMMIC.

A PEACEFUL RUN THROUGH THE ANCHORAGE.

I'VE HEARD OF DOGS LOOKING LIKE THEIR MASTERS BUT
THIS IS THE FIRST TIME I'VE SEEN A BOAT LOOK LIKE IT'S CAPTAIN.

53

ALWAYS PREPARED, THE CAPTAIN CAME WITH ANCHORS FOR EVERY BOTTOM.

"LET'S BUY A NICE QUIET PLACE DOWN BY THE WATER YOU SAID. YOU NEGLECTED TO TELL ME IT WAS ON THE I.C.W.!"

NO, MR. VLAD, WE'RE NOT INTERESTED IN COMING ABOARD FOR A LITTLE BITE, WE'RE ONLY INTERESTED IN SEEING YOUR VESSEL'S DOCUMENTS.

IT WAS PAYBACK TIME FOR MINI THE POODLE
AFTER WEEKS OF YAPPING.

NOW THAT I *SEE* IT PAINTED GREEN, I THINK IT LOOKED BETTER IN BLUE.

64

I KNOW YOU'RE NEW TO BOATING SWEETIE BUT THE KING SIZE HIDE-A-BED YOU BOUGHT HAS TO GO!

SHORTY AND THE MISSIS SOLD THEIR TRAWLER LESS THAN A YEAR AGO...BUT OLD HABITS DIE HARD!

ALWAYS ONE TO SAVE A BUCK, CAPTAIN BOB IMPALES HIMSELF ON THE SALON WINDOWS WHILE SELF-INSPECTING HIS 6-MAN LIFE RAFT.

I'VE NOTICED YOU CAN ALWAYS TELL WHO HAS STABILIZERS ABOARD AFTER BEING OUT ON ROUGH WATER.

VELCOME TO OUR DARK LITTLE BAY. VE'D BE HONORED IF YOU'D JOIN US UP AT THE CASTLE FOR A BITE... SAY ABOUT MIDNIGHT?

GOOD HEAVENS... IT'S TRUE!

HARRY!! THERE ARE PEOPLE OUT HERE WANTING TO SEE OUR HOLY PLACE?...THEY COME FROM AFAR....

AFFIRMATIVE... I AM YOUR ASSIGNED DELIVERY CAPTAIN HERE TO PILOT YOUR VESSEL NORTH.

SO MUCH FOR LEAVING THE TRAPPINGS OF CIVILIZATION BEHIND.

IT'S MY OPINION THAT THE JOY OF ANCHORING IS USURPED ONLY BY BEING TIED TO THE DOCK, HENCE MY PREDISPOSITION TO REMAINING AT THE MARINA.

84

85

86

87

88

89

SEGWAY UNDER WAY.

AN INTRODUCTION TO "ISLAND TIME".

WITH THE HIGH COST OF FUEL AND BOAT INSURANCE,
FRANK AND DEE FOUND OTHER WAYS TO ENJOY BOATING!

THE JOY OF NEW EQUIPMENT BEGINS WITH PROGRAMMING.

YOU SAID YOU HAD TO HAVE A PRIVATE SPACE TO GET AWAY FROM ME AND READ... I'VE REFITTED THE ANCHOR LOCKER JUST FOR YOU HON!

95

"A CLASSIC TRAWLER"